© 2025 by Quarto Publishing Group USA Inc.

First published in 2025 by Rock Point, an imprint of The Quarto Group,
142 West 36th Street, 4th Floor, New York, NY 10018, USA
(212) 779-4972 www.Quarto.com

All rights reserved. No part of this book may be reproduced in any form without written permission of the copyright owners. All images in this book have been reproduced with the knowledge and prior consent of the artists concerned, and no responsibility is accepted by producer, publisher, or printer for any infringement of copyright or otherwise, arising from the contents of this publication. Every effort has been made to ensure that credits accurately comply with information supplied. We apologize for any inaccuracies that may have occurred and will resolve inaccurate or missing information in a subsequent reprinting of the book.

Rock Point titles are also available at discount for retail, wholesale, promotional, and bulk purchase. For details, contact the Special Sales Manager by email at specialsales@quarto.com or by mail at The Quarto Group, Attn: Special Sales Manager, 100 Cummings Center Suite 265D, Beverly, MA 01915 USA.

10 9 8 7 6 5 4 3 2 1

ISBN: 978-1-57715-503-4

Digital edition published in 2025
eISBN: 978-0-7603-9406-9

Group Publisher: Rage Kindelsperger
Editorial Director: Erin Canning
Creative Director: Laura Drew
Managing Editor: Cara Donaldson
Editor: Nicole James
Text: Sara Weiss
Cover and Interior Illustrations: Lauren Mortimer
Cover and Interior Design: Evelin Kasikov

Library of Congress Cataloging-in-Publication Data

Names: Weiss, Sara (Writing consultant), author.
Title: A Frenchie life : what to know and love about the French bulldog / by Sara Weiss.
Description: New York, NY : Rock Point, an imprint the Quarto Group, 2025. | Includes bibliographic references. | Summary: "A Frenchie Life is a gorgeously illustrated guide to French bulldogs that explores the breed's loveable traits and provides helpful tips for every owner"-- Provided by publisher.
Identifiers: LCCN 2024041767 (print) | LCCN 2024041768 (ebook) | ISBN 9781577155034 (hardcover) | ISBN 9780760394069 (eISBN)
Subjects: LCSH: French bulldog--Popular works. | French bulldog--Pictorial works.
Classification: LCC SF429.F8 W45 2025 (print) | LCC SF429.F8 (ebook) | DDC 636.72--dc23/eng/20241107
LC record available at https://lccn.loc.gov/2024041767
LC ebook record available at https://lccn.loc.gov/2024041768

Printed in China

This book provides general information on various widely known and widely accepted images of dog breeds and pet ownership. However, it should not be relied upon as recommending or promoting any specific diagnosis or method of treatment for a particular condition a dog or pet may have, and it is not intended as a substitute for medical advice or for direct diagnosis and treatment of a medical condition by a qualified physician. Readers who have questions about a particular dog or pet condition, possible treatments for that condition, or possible reactions from the condition or its treatment should consult a veterinarian or other qualified healthcare professional. For entertainment and educational purposes only.

A FRENCHIE LIFE

What to Know and Love about the French Bulldog

Sara Weiss

Dedication

To Mom and Dad

Introduction 9

Frenchie Talk 15

Drama Queens 27

Attention Hogs 39

Silliness 47

Princess and the Pea 59

Super Affectionate 71

Stubbornness 85

Couch Potatoes 93

Love Bombs 105

Finding the Perfect Name for Your Frenchie 118
Taking Care of Your French Bulldog 120
Frenchie Resources 124
Acknowledgments 126
About the Author 127

Introduction

French bulldogs have climbed the ranks in popularity over time. According to the American Kennel Club (AKC), they recently claimed the esteemed spot as the top purebred dog in the United States, taking the crown from Labrador retrievers, who held the title for thirty-one years. They are considered the "it" dog and are quite a status symbol. So, what is it about French bulldogs that have captured so many hearts, propelling them to number one? Is it their bat ears? Their smushed and wrinkled faces? Their stocky little bodies? Their clownish antics and serious expressions?

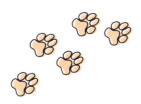

To understand what makes them so loveable, it helps to know a bit about where they have come from. The French bulldog derives from Britain's native bulldog, a breed used in the early part of the nineteenth century. These dogs were used for bullbaiting, or the brutal practice of pitting a dog against a bull in a vicious fight with spectators wagering on the outcome. Thankfully, animal combat was banned in the 1830s, and around this time, bulldogs started making their way into the show ring. They were divided by size, with the smallest breed then known as the English or toy bulldog.

During the Industrial Revolution, these smaller English bulldogs made their way to France in the arms of female lacemakers from Nottingham, who crossed the English Channel looking for work. The silly, spunky little dogs (known as *bouledogue Français*) gained popularity at many levels of French society, including among aristocrats, "ladies of the night" in Montmartre, writers, painters, and fashion designers.

Finally, American tourists brought these English/French bulldogs to the United States, where they further developed the breed with the erect bat ears and snub noses that we have come to know today. French bulldogs differ from modern English bulldogs in that they are smaller in stature, and they can cuddle on your lap much more easily than their English Bulldog friends, who take up way more space. Frenchies are also known for having much more energy than the more chilled out English bulldog.

Today, French bulldogs have smooth, brilliant coats and can come in a variety of colors including brindle, cream, white, black, and fawn.

A French bulldog's eye color can be shades of light or dark brown, blue, or green. They might have a "mask" over their nose and mouth or be "maskless."

Frenchies are on average 11–13 inches (28–33 cm) tall, weigh less than 28 pounds (13 kg), and generally live between ten and twelve years. Their trademark feature is their bat ears, and they also have large, square heads, wrinkles, folds, and short noses. Their bodies are short, compact, and muscular.

French bulldogs, also known as Frenchies, are playful, sweet, hilarious, silly, affectionate, and lovable—characteristics that make them the perfect companions. They appeal to people of all ages and are known for being family dogs who are generally good with kids and other animals. Their small size and the fact that they don't require a great deal of exercise make them adaptable to many environments and ideal for apartment living. They also look fabulous in clothing, can be tucked into a chic doggie duffle bag and are highly "Instagrammable." There are even an impressive number of Frenchie influencers out in the world.

Known for their silly antics as "clown dogs," "frog dogs," and "clowns in the cloak of a philosopher," French bulldogs bring joy and laughter into our lives. They like to "talk," making funny sounds to engage with people, and they sometimes skitter and zoom around with a toy in their mouth, ready for the chase. They are our little couch potatoes, enjoying a good snooze on the couch or in the sun. They also love to bask in the warmth of their favorite people and like to be as close to you as they can be, even if that means taking a nap on your chest—or on your face.

If you are considering bringing a French bulldog into your home, you should get to know all there is to know about this unique breed to make sure this is the right dog for you. French bulldogs can be quite stubborn, attention-seeking, dramatic, and occasionally mischievous. Because they are so attached to their humans, they can also be prone to separation anxiety, so they're not suited to being left alone for long periods.

Frenchies also have health issues that need to be closely monitored. These include breathing problems (because, like other brachycephalic breeds such as pugs, they have been bred to have cute, flat faces), allergies, skin problems, and a tendency to easily overheat. This means they don't make for the best running or outdoor adventure buddies, if that's what you are looking for, and you'll probably need to spend time and money on vet visits.

But if you are looking for a compact, silly companion who wants to be there by your side, a bowling ball of a dog who makes you laugh all day, and a snuggle muffin who nuzzles you when you're sad and lives for your attention and love, well then, a French bulldog is the pup for you.

Frenchie Talk

You might find that your **Frenchie** is never at a loss for words. We **love** our funny **friends** because they are not afraid to join the conversation or vocalize their displeasure.

You'll never feel alone when your **Frenchie is around.** Here are just a few ways a Frenchie talks.

The Grunt-Snort

Because of their short muzzles, recessed noses, soft palate, and large tongues, Frenchies tend to make interesting noise when they breathe. We can call it the grunt-snort. It sounds like the guttural rumbling sound a pig makes when dinner is served. Sometimes this noise is involuntary, and sometimes they do it on purpose to get our attention.

If your Frenchie is grunt-snorting to get your attention, they are probably trying to let you know you haven't spent quite enough time focusing on them. You've been so busy lately, poking your finger at that little electronic rectangle you always hold in your hand. The grunt-snort often goes along with a toy dropped at your feet and the classic Frenchie stare—head tilted with buggy, pleading eyes. You can engage in a grunt-snort conversation with your Frenchie and have a nice back-and-forth, but what they're really looking for is action, not just empty words.

The Warble

You don't necessarily think of small dogs with bat ears when you think of warblers, but Frenchies can really belt it out. They make a high-pitched sound like a mixture between a rooster's crow and a baby's cry that sounds like *Ar arrr*! They might sit in your lap as they do it, or they might do it during alone time—close to you, of course, because Frenchies are never far. As they say, "Sing like no one's listening and dance like nobody's watching." That's your Frenchie's motto.

The Chatterbox

If you're in a place where a lot people are conversing, such as a coffee shop or a subway car, your Frenchie might also want to talk. If they could make the same sounds we make, they would, but they are limited to certain mouth movements and vocal cord variations. That doesn't stop them! In their attempt to join in, though, your Frenchie might actually bring the conversation to a halt. Everyone is going to be a little curious about why your big-eyed baby dog is screaming a throaty *Uhwuwuwuwah!* Your Frenchie, performing a scintillating monologue, will be so in the moment that they won't even notice everyone's laughter.

Pupparazzi!

Frenchies tend to steal people's hearts left, right, and center. This happens so much that there is a whole tribe of super-famous Frenchies out there with millions of followers, sponsorships, and likely their own real estate portfolios!

Meet Milo Lu, a.k.a Frenchiebutt: We all have our talents and unique gifts, and Milo Lu's just happens to be napping. The little cream-colored French bulldog has earned international attention for his sleepy poses and expressions. He has hundreds of thousands of followers on Instagram. Milo Lu's mom and dad have photographed him falling asleep in their home in Seattle while wrapped in fluffy blankets; with his butt up, his head resting on his paws; and with his eyes and little ears poking out from atop a pillow. It's his smile that really gets you, though—it's a wide, serene grin that stretches across his little round noggin. We either have it or we don't—and there's no question Milo Lu was born a star.

The Howl

Some Frenchies howl like a kettle. They might do this while sitting and looking wistfully out a rain-splattered window, eyes closed and snout lifted. Maybe they are awaiting your return or communicating with Fido as he trots by. They might also howl to alert you that a storm is coming. They are trying to tell you, "Grab an armful of doggy biscuits and meet me under the bed in five."

The Symphony

In your very own home, you will get to enjoy a symphony of dog noises—a cacophony of syncopated rhythms and sounds that come out of your dog, letting you know they are near. Greatest hits include the bark, whine, slurp, snort, snuffle, purr, wheeze, reverse sneeze, and snore.

Now we need to have a little talk about one common sound that doesn't come from their front end. Yes, you can expect a fair amount of flatulence from your Frenchie. These food lovers have big appetites and often scarf down their meals a little too fast, which makes them take in some extra air. Your Frenchie will most likely do a lot of tooting, and that is just part of their charm.

Guest Star

Sunny the Frenchie! One very vocal French bulldog, Sunny, has become a bit of a celebrity in Amsterdam. One day, after living with his owners, Mary and Ortzy, for seven years, he started "talking" on the way to the vet. He engaged in a long conversation with them, letting out the strangest sounding, melodic, throaty sounds. And once he found his voice, there was no stopping him. When he is happy or excited, he blabs to those around him. He enjoys rolling around in a stroller, sometimes wearing outfits such as a wool hat, a bandana, or a fuzzy coat. A viral video of him on a crowded subway shows passengers laughing hysterically at the little dog in a stroller yammering away for all to listen. "He's just perfect," Mary says. "We would never change anything about him."

Drama Queens

French bulldogs love to get **positive attention,** but if they don't get what they want, they're not shy about letting their feelings be known. They can launch into quite the **Oscar-worthy performance** when they don't get their way. It comes from their deep emotional connection to us. They **love us so profoundly** that when we tell them something they don't want to hear, such as "that's enough dehydrated meat for now," it hurts. It really hurts! And if they have to whine a little bit or follow us to make sure we know they're still there and that they, too, have feelings—they will do that. Here are some of the ways our little **drama queens** like to express their emotions.

Please!

It is only fair and only kind of you to consider your Frenchie's feelings when you are cooking some aromatic, savory poultry in a pan in the kitchen. How is it fair for you to eat whenever you feel like it while they are limited to morsels of kibble twice a day? Life is about enjoying simple pleasures! Invoking the senses! Expanding the mind through the sensations and flavors of food in the mouth!

Your Frenchie can communicate all of this by positioning themselves beside your feet and striking just the right pose–ears upright, paws perfectly placed side by side, eyes unblinking, tongue licking their lips. If you see how desperate they are and how grateful they would be for just the tiniest taste, you might be compelled to drop some mozzarella on the floor. And if that doesn't work, they can always hope for happy accidents and the promise of fallen crumbs.

The Faux Faint

When you put on your shoes and grab your car keys, your French bulldog might lift their little head and howl. When you go to open the door, they may even go so far as to lean and topple over in distress like a Victorian lady. *How could you leave me? Woe is me!* They'll lie there, feet in the air—a winning performance. And because you're so enamored with them, you'll probably check their pulse, make sure they are breathing, and then give them some scratches and kisses before you go.

The Tantrum

Frenchies are not so good at taking constructive feedback, but who is? You accidentally drop a pillow on the floor, and your Frenchie assumes it is a new stuffie "for me!" When you find your Frenchie contentedly tearing it open with their teeth, white fuzz scattered across the floor and sticking to their mouth like a beard, you say, "Leave it." And then you take the pillow away.

They are wide-eyed, truly and utterly stunned, and frankly, pretty disappointed in your choices. The pillow was dropped by you, and since it was technically your fault, have you ever considered that maybe *you* should be the one to "Leave it"?

If whines, yips, and howls don't work, they'll have to turn their back on you with head askew, glancing back at you every once in a while just to make sure you see how deprived they are, until you can fully comprehend the injustice of the whole situation. Not even an "I'm sorry" will cut it as long as that pillow remains out of reach.

Watchdogs

Even though they are sweet, small, and squishy, French bulldogs make for surprisingly effective watchdogs. They have the same protective and territorial instincts that much larger dogs do, and they are known for their loyalty to and protectiveness of the ones they love. When a stranger is approaching your doorstep, your Frenchie will alert you by barking their head off, possibly leaping and skittering around the room to make sure you know what's up. Once the stranger has crossed the threshold into your home, though, your Frenchie will most likely drop the pretense and greet them with licks and love. Maybe they're better at watching than guarding—still, it's nice to know they're on the lookout.

The Sulk

You need to get work done and don't have time to play? After your French bulldog has tried subtly dropping a toy at your feet, resting a paw on your leg, and doing their best pathetic head tilt, they will sulk like a teenager. They'll snuffle and huff and wrinkle their little nose. They'll lay their heads on their paws with eyes lifted at you and let out the biggest sigh. Finish up whatever you're doing so you can scoop your Frenchie up in your arms and get outside for some playtime, a spring in both of your steps.

Hollywood Stars

French bulldogs have taken the stage for years, appearing in television shows such as *Modern Family* and in movies such as *Titanic* and *Due Date* with Zac Galifianakis. A number of dog-loving celebrities have also caught Frenchie fever. Reese Witherspoon loves her four furry friends and has posted pictures of herself snuggling with her black and white French bulldog, Minnie. Martha Stewart is known for her ever-growing family of Frenchies including, Luna Moona, Bette Noire, and Crème Brulee. The couple Chrissy Teigen (a self-proclaimed "dog mom") and John Legend (who once officiated a dog wedding) adopted an adorable three-legged Frenchie named Penny, who joined three other dogs in their family. Lady Gaga has owned a family of three Frenchies—Koji, Gustav, and Miss Asia. Dwayne "The Rock" Johnson is famous not only for saving the day in action movies, but also for jumping into a pool fully clothed to rescue Brutus, one of his Frenchie twins. The other twin, Hobbs, is a movie star too; he starred with Johnson in the 2019 film *Fast & Furious Presents: Hobbs & Shaw*. Hobbs also likes to join The Rock for workouts in the gym.

Attention Hogs

Frenchies are bred to be sociable **companion dogs,** and more than anything they thrive on human interaction. Because of this, they might go above and beyond to get you to notice them. They will strut over with a toy in their mouth, letting you know that the time for play is *now*! Or they will gaze into your soul with those expressive puppy eyes—you, the one they adore. There's nothing quite like the **classic Frenchie stare**.

Frenchies have a few clever tactics to get you to notice them. They will paw at you or nuzzle against you to remind you, "Hey, your cuddles are much appreciated." They'll roll around on their back to let you know you better keep those belly rubs coming. Maybe it's their Frenchie talk, a mix of yips and whines, or sometimes howls, that grabs your attention. Their **sweet** and **endearing** personalities are hard to resist, and with their smushed faces and silly energy, they make the **best company.** Here are just a few of their attention-seeking behaviors.

Please Don't Go!

"You weren't thinking about leaving the house, were you? Without moi?" When our little attention hogs don't get the attention they seek, they can get a little lonely. French bulldogs are prone to separation anxiety. Don't be surprised to hear from your neighbors about the excessive barking coming from your place while you were out. Your Frenchie might even scratch a hole in the wall in an attempt to get outta there and find you, wherever you are. Without you there to entertain them, what are they to do other than to pace around in boredom awaiting your return? You might come home to discover your furry friend has gotten into some mischief and trashed the place. There might even be canine teeth marks in your favorite shoes, or couch cushions might be torn to shreds. Picture the look of innocence—tilted head, wide eyes, and that classic Frenchie frown—you are sure to see.

To stave off separation anxiety, make the house a relaxing and exciting place for your Frenchie to be. Play some classic jams. Leave a doggy-safe chewy or Kong ball—everything is better with snacks. If you're going to be out for a long while, arrange for someone to come over and hang out with your Frenchie. Or, if you want to make it a real house party, why not bring a second Frenchie into your home to keep them company? Double the trouble, double the love!

Velcro Dogs

At least you'll receive a warm welcome when you return. Your Frenchie will be so happy to see you, they'll follow you everywhere to make sure you never ever *ever* think about leaving again. Affectionately dubbed "Velcro dogs," Frenchies are known to be a little clingy. You may discover a little shadow trailing you to the bathroom, a wet nose on your ankles on your way to get a snack, or the sound of paws behind you as you go to change the laundry. View it as a sign of love!

Please Sir, May I Have Some More?

Frenchies are so emotionally attached to you, they know just how to tug at your heartstrings to get you to go ahead and give them that food. You can try to be coy and steal a nighttime snack of salty chips, but you can't sneak one past them. No matter how quiet you think you are, you'll hear that familiar jingling and nails scrabbling against the tile floor, and you'll find a bat-eared Frenchie at your feet, giving you their best sad eyes to make you question your choices. Don't forget, you are the human! Yes, their mesmerizing, pathetic eyes are hard to resist. It would be so easy to just drop a little piece of your turkey sandwich on the floor to bring them temporary but acute joy. Don't do it! Set those boundaries, letting mealtime be mealtime, and you'll all be better for it in the long run.

Quality Time

- Spend some quality time with your Frenchie, and you'll both be bonded and happy. Romp around together! Play tug-of-war and fetch! Take a little stroll—but watch out for the paparazzi. (Sorry to break it to you, but they are most interested in your little friend.)

- Provide your pup with interactive and mentally stimulating toys. Train your Frenchie to understand simple commands, using positive reinforcement to keep them motivated and engaged. Make sure to shower your Frenchie with tons of cuddles to fill their cup and help them release anxiety. Snuggle sessions will build trust and foster the bond between you.

- Enjoy a daily stroll and romp around together. Exercise can help reduce stress, and it can help your Frenchie feel tuckered out so they are more relaxed for the rest of the day.

- Seek the help of a trainer or visit the vet if you feel like your Frenchie is anxious or extra hungry for attention.

- Although Frenchies can be a little needy at times, it'll be more than worth it. Kisses from a soft, big-eyed pup are truly a welcome distraction. A well-adjusted, happy French bulldog will be friendly and affectionate and show unconditional love. And when you're there to dole out attention and love, you'll be met with endless puppy adoration. Snores in your face, a bully butt cozying up to your feet, and a barrage of Frenchie licks... these are all ways for your Frenchie to let you know, "You are my number one."

Silliness

It can be hard to see the **beauty** and **lightness** in life when we're bogged down by stress. We might take ourselves too seriously and forget to laugh. One solution: find a Frenchie! Nothing brings more **silly energy** into your life than a goofy little pup with a scrunchy face. Dogs bring us joy and entertain us when we need it most—especially little bat-eared frog dogs with a **zest for life.** Thank goodness for French bulldogs! They are emotionally intelligent enough to sense when we could use a little cheering up and embrace their role as clown dogs.

The look of them is enough to **make you smile:** square heads, buggy eyes, stocky little bodies, smushed faces, and hilarious pouts. Not to mention, the French bulldog has some of the best moves on the **dance floor!** The way they move their little bodies can make them look like they belong in a Pixar movie, with each little wriggle and shake more ridiculous than the one before. Here are just a few of their silly and wacky antics

The Zoomies

Your French bulldog is amped! You've just returned home, a random houseguest has arrived, your Frenchie has emptied their bowels, or they've made it through a very trying experience such as bathtime and are filled with relief to be on the other side. It's Zoomie Time! Ready, set, *go*! When something more than exciting is about to happen, has just happened, or is happening, Frenchies zoom around the room in circles, *fast, fast, fast*. They channel their inner gremlin as they scamper panting and grunting, and there's nothing you can do except watch in awe as this spectacle takes place before your eyes.

Frog Dog

Sometimes the best way to get comfortable is to lie down and spread your hind legs out behind you like a frog. It's pretty nice to sprawl out with one's belly on the cool floor. That's what French bulldogs think, anyway. They've earned the silly nickname "frog dog" for this signature pose. It's also called a *sploot*. You should try it sometime!

Army Crawl

Once you're in a proper frog dog stance, you'll be in the perfect position to "army crawl." First, stay low like a soldier keeping out of the line of fire. Then slither around the room on your belly. Frenchies love to get around this way. They can snag all kinds of random bits of delectable crumbs with their face so close to the ground. It's also a really effective front- and hind-leg work out!

Colors and Patterns Galore!

French bulldogs are adored not only for their calm demeanor and small size, but also for their varied and distinctive coats. If you're not sure how to tell the difference between a brindled sable and a merle lilac, the following terminology might come in handy.

Let's talk about pattern

- **Brindle:** A striping effect on the coat. This is the most common coat pattern for a French bulldog.
- **Pied:** Colorful spots on a white base coat.
- **Merle:** Random splotches of colors.
- **Sable:** A tan or fawn-colored coat interspersed with black-tipped hairs.
- **Tan points:** A pattern with lighter socks, chest, eyebrows, and cheeks over the base coat color.
- **Solid pattern:** A solid-colored coat with no other pattern.

Now on to colors

- **Cream:** White, more rarely with a yellow or orange tint.
- **Black:** A solid, fully pigmented coat color.
- **Blue:** A rare bluish tinted gray color.
- **Chocolate:** Light brown.
- **Cocoa:** Dark brown.
- **Lilac:** A combination of blue and cocoa.
- **Isabella:** A combination of blue and chocolate.

There's an ongoing debate between "preservationists" and "inclusive breeders" about the definition of "standard" Frenchie colors and patterns. The official AKC Frenchie colors are variations of white, cream, fawn, and brindle (streaks of these lighter and darker colors twisted together). French bulldogs must be only those colors to be shown at dog shows backed by the AKC and French Bull Dog Club of America.

Preservationists insist on maintaining and breeding to these particular standards and preventing "fad colors" from entering elite dog shows. Inclusive breeders, on the other hand, believe there is a place for all varieties and colors of French bulldogs within the community.

The debate raises questions about the ethics of breeding "designer dogs" and about what practices will result in the best overall health of the breed. It also stirs up concerns about the potential discrimination behind some of the campaigns to keep DQ (disqualified) colors from entering the ring.

While non-standard or "fad" Frenchies are unwelcome in elite dog shows, (in fact, on the French Bull Dog Club of America's website, there's a "No Fad Colors" logo, a blue dog struck through with a red line), these pups are coveted by some dog lovers and can be more expensive than those that come in "classic" colors.

Clown Dog

Yet another affectionate nickname used to describe our Frenchie's eccentric demeanor: the "clown dog." Don't let that stern, upside-down mouth fool you: They are natural comedians. Some folks even refer to French bulldogs as "a clown in the cloak of a philosopher" due to the comedic nature behind their serious resting face. Not even kidding!

They are hilarious, even when they don't mean to be, in the way they stand with feet splayed, broad chest, sad eyes, and a frown on those serious, wrinkled, folded faces. They wiggle their bully butts at mealtime and do a jerky dance. They talk to us with vigor, though we don't always know what they are trying to say.

We take them seriously by showing them our devoted love and respect, but there is going to be a whole lot of laughter with a French bulldog in the house. Thank you, universe, for Frenchies.

Toto Was Supposed to Be a French Bulldog!

Rumor has it that in the movie *The Wizard of Oz*, the little dog Toto was a Cairn Terrier, but the illustrator of Frank L. Baum's book *The Road to Oz*, John R. Neill, originally drew him as a French bulldog. Neill supposedly based Toto on his own little Frenchie named Quinn. Allegedly, a French bulldog was cast to take the role in the movie, but in classic Frenchie style, was a little too stubborn to take direction and was recast.

Princess and the Pea

Taking good care of your pup is a way for you to show your **unconditional devotion** to them. You'll clean the dirt between their skin folds and wrinkles and scoop their poop. You'll take them to the vet for check-ups to keep them healthy. You'll cool them down when they overheat, play with them, keep them mentally engaged, and feed them a **healthy diet**. You'll do all of this because of the love you feel for your companion. French bulldogs are a little more sensitive to the elements than some other breeds, requiring a bit of maintenance, and a caring owner who is willing to keep them healthy and happy. But the **adoration** you'll get in return can't be measured. They are one of a kind! Here are some of the things you'll do for love.

Clean Skin-Fold Gunk

Yup. You think you'll mind doing this, but you won't! You'll take a warm, damp washcloth and clean your Frenchie's face folds and wrinkles to prevent any pungent bacteria and yeast from growing there, and then you'll use a towel to gently pat them dry. You don't want gunk to get trapped in your Frenchie's face folds, do you? After that's done, you'll check the pocket of skin under your French bulldog's tail, too. When it comes down to it, aren't we all looking to find that special someone to clean smelly bacterial growths out of our face folds, wrinkles, and tail pockets? That's what love's all about.

Feed Them a Special Frenchie Diet

Because of their breathing problems, tendency toward obesity, and food allergies, you'll be feeding your French bulldog a specialized diet with nutritionally rich meals full of high-quality proteins that are easy to digest. Maybe you will need to ship a freeze-dried meal of specialty lamb and mustard greens from a valley in the Swiss Alps, and maybe you will need to sell your car and eat ramen every day to support them, but you will do it for love.

Manage Their Temperature (Un)Control

French bulldogs can be a little bit like the princess from "The Princess and the Pea." They are sensitive to the elements. The cold *does* bother them because of their short fur and compact nasal structure. A winter wardrobe might be in order, and you'll need to limit their time outside in frigid temps.

Overheating is also an issue for Frenchies, as it is for many flat-faced brachycephalic breeds, but that doesn't stop them from soaking up the rays. Frenchies love to bake like a potato in the sun. You'll help manage their temperature by limiting their sun time, fanning them off when necessary, giving them sponge baths, and pretty much tending to them like they're royalty. (Just don't feed them grapes of luxury! Grapes are toxic for dogs, even in small numbers.)

Emotional Support Dogs

French bulldogs are the perfect pets to offer companionship and support to those who need it most. Although some French bulldogs can work as service dogs, they are suited best to help people with certain disabilities. Because of their small stature, they wouldn't be the best choice to help someone with mobility issues or to be a guide dog for someone who is blind. But what they can offer is emotional support due to their sweet and calm demeanor, adaptability, and emotional intelligence. They are an ideal breed to work as emotional support and therapy dogs, providing comfort to their handler during an anxiety attack, bringing medication to their owner, or alerting someone with hearing loss to alarms. Although they are highly trainable for this kind of work, they can be quite stubborn, as we know, so they might require a little extra oomph and persistence in the form of yummy treats and praise to pass the test.

Watch Out for Water

To help with their overheating, you might provide your Frenchie with a cooling mat, give them a wet bandana, or let them splash around in a kiddie pool. Just keep an eye on them and give them a doggy life vest! They're no Michael Phelps. Although they'll need to cool off to keep from overheating, they will also need to be surveilled closely around any body of water because they are not good swimmers. They are top heavy, meaning they have large, heavy heads that can make them topple forward or sink in the water. And with their flat snouts, thick muscles, and heavy bones, they are not built to be aquatic. Hey, that's okay! We all have our strengths and weaknesses.

Become Besties with the Veterinarian

We have talked about the number of health issues that a Frenchie can have because of the way they have been bred. We've got brachycephalic obstructive airway syndrome, heatstroke, sensitive skin, chronic ear infections, cataracts, hip dysplasia—and you get the idea. You should plan to spend a lot of time at your veterinarian's office over the next decade or more, which could be a pretty big financial commitment. And it's also probably a good idea for you to get to know your veterinarian on a more personal level to receive the best care. If your vet has any hobbies—such as golfing, gaming, knitting, or gardening—you should take up those hobbies now. I would also suggest learning if they have any nicknames. And get your holiday card out to them early so they can hang it somewhere highly visible to all visitors in the waiting room. Always a good idea to get on their best side.

An Aristocratic Past

In Paris, French bulldogs (*bouledogue Français*) were highly aristocratic and fashionable pets, sought out by ladies in high society as well as by "ladies of the night," writers, painters, and fashion designers. French artists Edgar Degas and Henri de Toulouse-Lautrec were thought to have depicted French bulldogs in their paintings. Degas's painting *At the Stables, Horse and Dog* features a large brown horse in a stable, standing next to what appears to be a little black and white French bulldog. Toulouse-Lautrec's painting *Bouboule* shows what looks like a black and white Frenchie, too.

Other noted owners of French bulldogs include the French fashion designer Yves Saint Laurent—and in America, the Rockefellers and J.P. Morgan. A French bulldog named Gamin de Pycombe even made it aboard the Titanic (but didn't survive the crossing, sadly).

Super Affectionate

Frenchie family, prepare yourself for snuggles! When they feel **bonded to you**, French bulldogs will show you the lovin'. They enjoy nothing more than nuzzling in close to their loved ones. These love bugs are especially **affectionate** because they were bred not to retrieve hunted ducks or to herd sheep or to track a scent, but to be, first and foremost, our *little wittle smushy wooshy bully babies*. In fact, some people find they are most **attracted** to French bulldogs as their pets because their features (flat snouts, big heads, warm compact bodies, and large expressive eyes) remind us of human babies. Or a cross between bunnies and babies. Furry little dog-bunny-babies.

Cuddles

French bulldogs are the best at cuddling: belly rubs with feet in the air, a nuzzle into your neck, a warm potato contentedly sighing at your feet while you're reading. Cuddles are good for you and for them. It's a symbiotic relationship!

Kisses

Wherever you go, you'll be covered in French bulldog saliva. They love to give you kisses! It's an instinct passed down to them through the generations, from their wolf ancestors. They lick to let you know, "Look, I'm not trying to be a threat." They'll even tolerate the occasional human style kiss, but they'd probably prefer we lick them back instead.

Goo-Goo Eyes

There's nothing quite like a loving gaze from a big-eyed baby-dog. French bulldogs like to stare fondly at their favorite person. They might sit on the floor with a little tilt of the head and watch what you're up to. Their ears move when you move. "I'm here," they are trying to tell you, "and I am yours."

Philanthro-PUP

Possibly the most famous Frenchie of them all, Manny the Frenchie amassed more than 1 million followers on social media in his lifetime. The black and white pup was the runt of the litter and on his way to a shelter when he was adopted by Amber Chavez and Jon Huang, who brought him to their home in Chicago to live with four furry siblings: Frank, Filip, Liam, and Leila. Manny became famous for his cute photos and videos: napping in the sink, falling asleep sitting up, jumping high for treats, rocking out with sunglasses, dressed up in crocs or a chef's hat, snuggling with his siblings, or engaging in some serious Frenchie talk to get his way. He also scored an author credit on his very own book, *Manny the Frenchie's Art of Happiness*, a humorous illustrated guide to living a happy and fulfilling life. But it was his passion for helping others that inspired people and pups around the world. Manny (with a bit of human help) visited children's hospitals, raised money for a dog shelter, helped rescue pups from puppy mills, and even started the Manny and Friends Foundation to help those in need.

Snoozey Snuggles

Wrap an arm around your Frenchie and take a nap—you'll wake up as refreshed and relaxed as if you've just had a massage or a salt bath. It's really good for the mood to fall asleep with a warm, snoring pocket of mushiness. You should feel honored if they choose to lie on your lap or on your chest, and especially if they choose to lie on your face. If you wake up with a French bulldog snoring on your face, good on you. That means that you are officially in the club. You have earned their trust. Bravo!

Playtime

Wiggly bums, bursts of energy, games of tug-of-war and fetch, and joyful wrestling—these are all ways your Frenchie is trying to let you know they trust you. Playfulness is one way your pup shows their affection. So get down on the floor and wrestle and wiggle your bum too! You know you want to!

Stress Busters

Doctor's orders: Cuddling with your dog will benefit your health. It's science! It can decrease stress hormones, lower blood pressure, and trigger the release of the happy hormone (oxytocin). The point is, dogs make us happy. It doesn't take science to tell us that, though, does it?

Bugsy and Malone

A nine-year-old French bulldog named Bugsy stepped in to take care of a baby orangutan named Malone after he was abandoned by his mother at the Twycross Zoo in England. The pair spent time nuzzling, napping together, holding hands, and even kissing each other on the lips. Soon, Malone was ready to join the other orangutans—but he couldn't have done it without the love and support of his Frenchie friend.

Stubbornness

Good luck trying to get a Frenchie to do something they don't want to do! They don't call 'em bulldogs for nothing! French bulldogs are **trainable**–as in, they are smart enough to learn the **tricks** and follow the **commands**– but they are also *stubborn*, meaning they'll only do it if it suits them. If they could talk, they might sound like Melville's "Bartleby the Scrivener": "I would prefer not to."

It's hard not to giggle when our Frenchies are turning their backs on us in passive resistance or yipping in protest because we won't give them what they want. They are just so **gosh darn cute.** How can we resist their little baby faces? They are such compact little creatures with **personality** in spades.

The Refusal

It's frigid outside and you need to take your Frenchie out to go to the bathroom. You would like to put a sweater on your pup, which seems reasonable to you. You manage to get the clothing over their flat-faced head and ears and pull their paws through the sleeves, but your Frenchie gives you a big-eyed, exasperated look letting you know how demeaning the sweater is. You click the leash on their collar and open the door to go, but your French bulldog won't budge. It's astonishing how difficult it is to move a dog whose body weight is only 6 percent of your own! You don't want to give in and let your small alien friend be the boss of you, but you'd also like to get on with your day, so you take the sweater off and they trot outside with you onto the crispy cold grass.

Catch Me If You Can

You're trying to finish up one last thing for work, just one last thing, while your Frenchie is not-so-subtly shaking a toy in their mouth and pawing at your calves. "Give me twenty minutes," you say. But the thing is, they are feeling like playtime *now*. In twenty minutes, they might want to take a little nap. They keep shaking the toy and let out a few little wrinkle-faced grunts. That's when you see the glint in their eye. They take your shoe in their mouth and bolt.

The next twenty minutes are no longer spent working, but instead chasing a dog around the room. Your Frenchie freezes and crouches with the shoe in their mouth, daring you. You take one gentle step in their direction, and the game begins again.

Then it's over. They drop the shoe, panting, looking up at you between gulps of water. And you are sweating and out of breath too.

Don't Let Your Pup Be the Boss of You!

- Always reward good behavior. Train your pup with positive reinforcements such as treats, compliments, and pets, being as clear and consistent as you can to let them know your expectations.

- If your Frenchie regularly likes to enjoy a game of "catch me if you can" with shoes, TV remotes, or wallets, make sure they are getting enough exercise before the thievery begins. If they're doing it for your attention, it might be best to ignore them until they drop the thing on their own. If you need to get the item away from them pronto, try a diversion tactic such as sprinkling treats in another room or ringing the doorbell.

- Try to ignore unwanted behaviors such as Frenchie tantrums and sulking, as cute as they might be. If your pup is a master at sulking, keep them engaged with food puzzles, snuffle mats, or the like for mental stimulation and to encourage independence. Provide them with lots of outdoor time (though not too much time in the sun) so they can enjoy all there is to sniff and to keep them engaged and happy.

Couch Potatoes

It is *extremely* distracting and difficult to get anything done when a **furry little snuggle bunny** is lounging about. And when it comes to lounging about, French bulldogs are *kings*. If there was an Olympic sport devoted to lounging about, French bulldogs would bring home the **gold.** They might not win any major awards for other athletic feats (because of—as previously discussed—their smushed-nose breathing problems and their potential to easily overheat). They might also lose the competition in following directions and listening to commands (because of their bullheadedness). But Frenchies are absolute **champions** when it comes to being a **couch potato.** (Cue the applause!) Here are some of their best couch potato poses, listed by ascending degree of difficulty.

The Snorer

This Olympic event definitely uses a French bulldog's natural skill set. Their brachycephaly, or narrow nostrils and short noses can lead to some serious respiratory issues that are no joke–but our little Frenchies do make some pretty funny noises such as snorts, snores, and grunts. To bring home the trophy, the pup needs to really let it rip as their belly rises and falls, snoring all of their cares away. They win extra points for cuteness if they snore so loudly that they accidentally startle and wake themselves up.

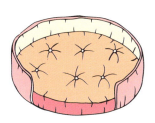

Superman

When they perform this trophy-winning position, your French bulldog will fall asleep in such a way that it looks as if they are soaring through the sky like a superhero. Before getting into position, they might need to stretch, shake, and shudder. Then they will lie down on their stomach, front legs forward and back legs behind them, and fly into dreamland.

The Barnacle

Your Frenchie will showcase their coach potato prowess by draping and planting themselves on your body as if you are a rock. To master this pose, both you and your Frenchie need to be in a complete Zen state of snoozing, while they are lying on your chest, your back, or even occasionally across your face. Zzzzz.

Bat Ears

It was once more common for Frenchies to have one of two different kinds of ears: "rose ears" or "bat ears." Rose ears fall to the side of a dog's head in a rounded shape, displaying some of the inside of the ear, whereas bat ears point upward and appear to be almost too large for the pup's head. In the early 1900s, Americans insisted that only bat ears should be considered as a modern breed standard. When they discovered that both were deemed valid at an exhibition in Westminster, the American judge refused to judge, and the Americans pulled their dogs out of the show. The French Bull Dog Club of America quickly formed, and fanciers officially redefined the breed standard, allowing for the bat ear and the bat ear only. Today, the erect bat ear is considered a Frenchie trademark feature.

The Octopus

The degree of difficulty here is very high. It might seem to you that your French bulldog has only four legs, but in the full expression of this position, they can give the impression of actually having eight. This is because of the way they can spread their bodies out, leaving you no room. Despite their petite, compact frames, they manage to plop down and take up the entire couch so that you must either sit on the arm or on the floor. Mad props to Frenchies for this one!

Sun Hog

Lastly, this is the pose with the highest degree of difficulty, and Frenchies must endure hours and hours of relentless training to master it. The first step is to find a sun spot to lie in, which is not easy to do! The sun moves through the day. You don't want to settle in for a warm nap on an armchair only to discover that the light has shifted and the spot has now moved onto the floor. Once your Frenchie chooses their spot, they must fully commit, contorting their body to rest in a very precarious spot in the middle of the staircase or curling into the last tiny triangle of light until the sun has set. It takes determination and grit to pull this off, and Frenchies are the ones to do it!

Comfort Queen

One special Frenchie named Hazel has provided comfort to many people by visiting schools, hospitals, and bereavement centers. Hazel and her handler, Sara Morgan, went through training at a PetSmart in San Antonio, learning commands and practicing them in different environments, including crowded and loud places. They were evaluated and certified as a therapy team. Hazel received awards as an American Kennel Club (AKC) Canine Good Citizen and AKC Therapy Dog. She was named the 2022 Pet Partners Pet of the Year—and *The AKC Family Dog Magazine* wrote an article about her, naming her the "Comfort Queen."

When Hazel wears her yellow vest, she knows she's on the job, and she's ready to lift a paw, give a kiss, or snuggle up to someone just to bring a smile to their face. She brings a moment of calm and joy to people who have experienced grief. At the hospital, she greets the nurses and then snuggles up to children, letting them give her pets while they get IVs, or sits beside them on their beds. Hazel charms everyone with her sweet brown eyes, soft fur, and small size, giving them a bit of solace in hard times.

Love Bombs

How does it feel to come home to an **emphatic,** wiggling Frenchie butt? Do you know anyone else who is *that* excited to see you? **The love is so real.** Loving your Frenchie is about how they make you feel, how much joy they bring into your life, and how **obsessed** you are with one another. We love them so much that we want to be with them, and we miss them dearly when they're not around. We love them so much that we will do anything to make sure they're okay. We love them so much that we occasionally like to close our eyes and lean in just to get a whiff of their warm, earthy scent. (Did I say that out loud? Dog lovers, come on—don't pretend like you don't know what I'm talking about.) French bulldogs have a lot of personality in their little bodies—so much **sassiness and humor.** They make us smile and laugh. We want to look after them and protect them. They are our best friends. Here are some of the things we do for them because we love them so.

Dress Them Up

Don't be the one to dull your Frenchie's sparkle. If they are a fashionista, let them shine. Whether they're into furry vests, ugly sweaters, snowman pajamas, hoodies, sunglasses, bucket hats with ear holes, or graphic tees featuring their favorite band, just let them be who they want to be. And you should be who you are too, especially if you are someone who enjoys coordinating your outfit with your dog's. You might consider hiring a photographer to follow the two of you as you trot around town—capturing those sepia-toned moments when you're both looking out wistfully at a duck pond in your matching overalls.

Take Them with You

We love to be around our Frenchies as much as they like to shadow us. French bulldogs are not quite small enough to be lap dogs you can carry around in your purse. However, some people do strap them to the front or back of their body in a dog carrier or push them around in a stroller and coo at them all day long. If your boss is up for it, bring your Frenchie to team meetings to have a say in the company's year-end plan. Bring them to lunch with your besties. Take them to Pilates class and Zumba. Everyone will love them, and that might even make them love you more.

Confide in Them

Frenchies are the best secret keepers! Tell them anything and they won't blab. Share your woes and fears and they'll comfort you. Give them all the hot gossip. Sing and they won't judge you. You'll find yourself talking to them as if they know exactly what you're saying, because they are there gazing at you, and they love you. They are very tuned in to us. Let them be your best friend and your confidant.

Pricey Pups

Although French bulldogs are low maintenance when it comes to their demeanor and exercise needs, they do tend to come at a high cost. French bulldogs cost an average of $1,500 to $3,000, but some people spend as much as $30,000! The price tag goes up based on responsible breeding, the color of the breed (rare shades such as blue, lilac, and chocolate cost more), the coat pattern (more for pied, merle, or brindle), eye color (more for blue eyes), and gender (females are more expensive than males.)

Why are they so expensive? As discussed, they are in demand for their small size and their friendly, funny, and affectionate demeanor. The cost is also due to the challenges of breeding French bulldogs. Because of their body shape and narrow hips, they're not built to safely mate on their own, instead requiring artificial insemination. Mothers must undergo a C-section to give birth because the breed's large head and wide shoulders make it difficult for her to birth her puppies naturally.

There are also the vet bills. We've discussed illnesses, allergies, breathing issues, and other challenges that come along with having little legs, big heads, and smooshed snouts.

And then, of course, there's the price people will pay for doggy fashion, keeping their Frenchie's wardrobe current. A Fendi dog jumper might just be an essential purchase.

They Love You Too

This will come as no surprise to dog lovers, but scientists have now confirmed that dogs experience a range of emotions, just as humans do. They feel emotions such as excitement, fear, anxiety, confusion, jealousy, calm, and joy. Brains scans of dogs show that specific areas of their brains respond to emotional triggers much in the same way that human brains do. So snuggle up with your pup to brighten your life—and theirs too.

Oldest Frenchie

The average lifespan of a Frenchie is ten to twelve years, but one black and white pup far outlived the norm. Rocco was one of the oldest French bulldogs ever recorded, making it to his eighteenth birthday before he passed away in 2024. Rocco's owner, Reuben Ford, believed Rocco's long life could be attributed to love, healthy foods, and lots of attention. Other than losing his hearing, he was in relatively good health until the end. Reuben believed that his longevity was also in part due to the fact that he was slimmer and had a longer muzzle than many "designer dogs." Born in São Paulo, Brazil, on February 1, 2006, Rocco spent his lifetime traveling the world, but in his older age, enjoyed lazy time in his home in Los Angeles snuggled up on the couch and watching movies.

Feel the Feels

Don't try to hide it: You are done for. You might not have known you were capable of such raw and visceral love for an alien fur ball, but here you are. Even when they're infuriating you with their stubbornness, grunting at you, zooming, tooting, or turning your place upside down like the Tasmanian Devil, you will find yourself in a blissful state when you are with them. You'll stare at them when they are sleeping, watching their belly rise and fall, laughing at how one of their ears has turned inside out, and marveling at just how little their paws really are.

They are our clown-dogs, our snuggle-bunnies, and our shadows. They are our goblins and our food lovers. They make us laugh all day with their toots and slobbers, their funny talk, their naps, their frog dog *sploots*, their teenage angst, and their snuggles. When we need somebody to love, there they are. They make us feel less alone. They are our playmates, our troublemakers, and our admirers and gazers. They are our best friends. They are our Frenchies.

Finding the Perfect Name for Your Frenchie

From French pastry-inspired to old-guard traditional to wildly charming, the name possibilities for a French bulldog are endless! Here are some of the most famous, most common, and most adorable options for Frenchie names.

Adèle

Adeline

Alfie

Alice

Alma

Ami/amie (Friend)

Anais

Andre

Antoine

Arthur

Baby

Baguette

Bale

Bear

Beau

Bernadette

Bisous

Blanchard

Bonaparte (Bonnie)

Boo

Broadway

Bunny

Button

Calvin

Camille

Cannoli

Céline

Chanel

Charles (Charlie)

Charlotte

Chase

Chauncey

Chéri (Darling)

Chloé

Claude

Coco

Coucou

Colette

Crème Brûlée

Croissant

Degas

Dior

Domino	Jean	Pip
Dottie	Joan of Arc	Pippa
Édith	Jules	Pistachio
Elise	King	Pomme (Apple)
Eloise	Léo	Porky
Emil	Louboutin	Prince
Fletcher	Louise	Princess
Floria	Madeleine	Queenie
Francie	Marcel	Quincy
Gabriel	Marie	Remy
Gaspard	Marion	Rocky
Georgie	Martini	Russell
Gouda	Max	Saint
Henri	Milo	Shadow
Hugo	Minnie	Simone
Hulk	Monet	Squishy
Ink	Olivia	Sugar
Iris	Olive	Tarte (Pie/Cake)
Isaac	Patate (Potato)	Teeny
Jackie	Pearl	Toulouse
Jaime	Pêche (Peach)	Victor
Jambon (Ham)	Peu (Little)	Violet
Jaq	Pierre	

Taking Care of Your French Bulldog

Health Considerations

- French bulldogs are prone to a variety of health issues such as breathing problems (common to flat-faced, or brachycephalic, breeds); overheating in hot weather; eye issues such as cherry eye, juvenile cataracts, or entropion; skin disorders; and allergies.

- They should never be left unattended near a body of water or a tub because they are not built for swimming.

- They are sensitive to anesthesia, like many flat-faced breeds.

- Be sure to check with the AKC to ensure that you are working with a responsible breeder who has the French bulldog's health, behavior, and stability in mind.

Recommended Health Tests from the National Breed Club

- Patella Evaluation
- Hip Evaluation

- Cardiac Exam
- Ophthalmologist Evaluation

Breed Information from the AKC

akc.org/dog-breeds/french-bulldog

The Offficial Breed Club Health Statement

frenchbulldogclub.org/health

Grooming

- Brush your Frenchie's short hair with a medium bristle brush, rubber grooming mitt, and hound glove to remove excess hair, promote new growth, and help to distribute oils throughout the coat.

- Clean and dry your Frenchie's facial folds and wrinkles and get under their tail as well.

- Trim your Frenchie's nails regularly.

Exercise

- French bulldogs enjoy a short walk with their owner, a play session such as tug-of-war or hide and seek, and agility or obedience training to keep their minds sharp.

- Because they have a tendency to overheat and due to their breathing difficulties, exercise and outdoor time should be limited, particularly in very hot or humid weather.

Training

- It's important to start socializing and training your French bulldog early to get them used to different situations and to help them grow into a well-behaved adult. Join a socialization and training puppy class in your area.

- Although French bulldogs are stubborn and tend to only follow directions when it suits them, they can be motivated by positive reinforcement such as treats and praise.

- Ultimately, Frenchies want to make their owners happy, and teaching them to follow commands and listen early on will help to foster a happy, balanced relationship between the two of you.

Nutrition

- French bulldogs require a well-balanced diet with high-quality proteins, fats, carbohydrates, vitamins, and minerals. Consider their calorie intake and monitor their weight, because Frenchies are prone to obesity, which can then lead to other health issues.

- They should be given treats in moderation.

- Avoid giving them table scraps when possible.

- Make sure all ingredients are dog safe, and always check with your vet with any questions about your pup's diet.

Frenchie Resources

According to American Kennel Club (AKC), "AKC Marketplace is the only site to exclusively list 100% AKC puppies from AKC-Registered litters and the breeders who have cared for and raised these puppies are required to follow rules and regulations established by the AKC." This website offers resources for purchasing French bulldog puppies from a breeder:

marketplace.akc.org/puppies/french-bulldog

French Bulldog Rescue Network (FBRN) is a resource for adopting rescued French bulldogs. On this site, you will find available dogs who deserve a second chance and a forever home. You can also reach out to this rescue if you are interested in fostering Frenchies, particularly those dogs who are sick, handicapped, or need expensive veterinary care before they can be placed for adoption—and consider sponsoring a foster to help offset these costs. Donations to FBRN are always welcome so they can continue to provide love and support to Frenchies who need it.

frenchbulldogrescue.org

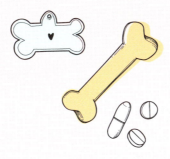

Acknowledgments

I would like to thank my editor, Nicole James, for her vision and enthusiasm, as well as Sarah O'Connor and the whole team at Quarto for helping to bring this series of books about dogs to life. Thanks to my friends and readers of my work over the years, fellow artists in the Cut and Paste ARIM (Artist Residency in Motherhood), my writing teachers at Sarah Lawrence College, Tufts, and Friends School. Thank you to my close friends who have been there, always, supporting my writing. You know who you are. Thanks to my childhood dog, Sparky, and to my sweet and silly Sato dog, Cali, who makes us laugh and brings us endless joy and love. Thank you to the hard working volunteers at Heaven Can Wait Rescue - Northstar Dogs for Adoption for bringing Cali to us. Finally, I would like to thank my family: my parents, Jan and Michael, and my sister, Rachel; my nieces, aunts, uncles, cousins, and in-laws. I'm forever grateful to my husband, Kevin, for his kindness, love, and support, and to my incredible daughters, Nora and Rosie, who will always have my heart.

About the Author

Sara Weiss holds an MFA from Sarah Lawrence College. She is the author of *A Labrador Life*, *A Golden Life*, and *The Totally Awesome World of Caitlin Clark*. Her writing has appeared in journals and magazines such as *Literary Mama*, *Mutha*, *Lilith*, *Waterwheel Review*, *Bustle* and *Brain Child*, among others. She has written audio scripts for *Good Night Stories for Rebel Girls* and works as a college writing consultant. She lives in the Hudson Valley with her husband, two daughters, and their little Sato rescue dog named Cali.

Who Can Have Just One Dog?

With so many breeds to love, collect and enjoy all the companion titles celebrating our favorite friends:

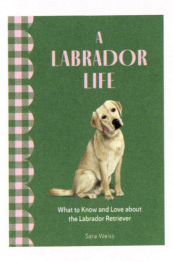

A Labrador Life

What to Know and Love about the Labrador Retriever

ISBN: 978-1-57715-504-1

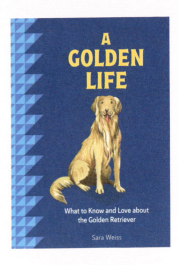

A Golden Life

What to Know and Love about the Golden Retriever

ISBN: 978-1-57715-502-7